Buffalo Bills IQ:
The Ultimate Test of True Fandom

Jim Baker

2012 Edition
(Volume I)

This title is part of the IQ sports trivia book series, which is a trademark of Black Mesa Publishing, LLC.

Cataloging-in-Publication Data is available from the Library of Congress.

ISBN: 978-0-9837922-7-7
First edition, first printing.

Cover photo courtesy of Mark Watmough.

Black Mesa Publishing, LLC
Florida
David Horne and Marc CB Maxwell
Black.Mesa.Publishing@gmail.com

www.blackmesabooks.com

Buffalo Bills IQ

I am dedicating this book to my wonderful wife Barbara, our four children – Kathleen, LeeAnn, Thomas and Erin and their families – along with our nine grandchildren.

Contents

Marv Levy, the inspirational coach who guided the Bills to an NFL-record four straight Super Bowls, had a game-day penchant for igniting his players with this moving declaration before they took the field for a huge showdown:

"Where else would you rather be than right here, right now?"

Introduction

IN **1960,** WHILE I was a student at the University of Buffalo and a strong football fan, a group of wealthy entrepreneurs decided to risk starting a new football league to challenge the National Football League's Monopoly.

They founded the American Football League and Ralph C. Wilson Jr. of Detroit decided to place his franchise in Buffalo, where the Bills exist today—more than a half-century later.

Buffalo emerged to become a thriving sports metropolis with the Bills joining the NHL Sabres, the minor-league baseball Bisons and for a while, the NBA Buffalo Braves.

The Bills have experienced the ups and downs of fortunes—before and since joining the NFL via the merger of 1970. Their successes can be divided into eras led by Lou Saban, who coached the Bills to two AFL championships, and Marv Levy, who guided them to four consecutive Super Bowls—a feat unmatched by any team.

The successes of their stars can also be divided into distinct eras—Jack Kemp and Daryle Lamonica, keys to Saban's first two title teams in 1964 and '65, and then Jim Kelly becoming the quarterback-engineer of those four Super Bowl teams with a passing arm that rewrote the team's record book.

The magical exploits of Doug Flutie and the record-breaking accuracy of Drew Bledsoe—after being acquired from New England—continued the Bills' winning tradition.

Through the years, the biggest winners have been the team's loyal fans—filling Ralph Wilson Stadium and, before that Rich Stadium and War Memorial Stadium, with incredible enthusiasm. Though Buffalo and Western New York form far from the largest fan base in America, the team's loyal followers have repeatedly shown the size of their hearts cannot be beaten!

I hope you enjoy following that tradition of success through this collection of Bills' history and trivia.

Jim Baker
August 2011

"I share this stage with some great football people. And the honor comes to one who never played the game. I play tennis. Because in tennis, folks, when you go back to serve, you don't have to worry about the rush of Bruce Smith."
— Ralph C. Wilson, Hall of Fame Induction Speech

Chapter One

Ralph C. Wilson

ONCE UPON A TIME, or rather 1959, a wealthy Detroit resident named Ralph C. Wilson Jr., joined Lamar Hunt, Bud Adams and several other prominent Americans with a strong interest in football to join in forming the American Football League. Wilson, who had a minority interest in the Detroit Lions, announced on October 17, 1959, that his fledgling franchise would be in Buffalo—and six weeks later he named it "the Bills."

The name was generated by a contest in 1946. The idea was to find a name for the All-America Conference team in Buffalo that would be distinguished from the minor league baseball and hockey "Bisons," and several among 4,500-plus entrants suggested the Bills, which won out over "Bullets," "Nickels" and "Blue Devils." James F. Dyson was selected the winner after writing that legendary Indian scout William "Buffalo Bill" Cody helped trail blaze the American Frontier and the Bills would launch a new frontier in Buffalo sports. Wilson chose the name and Dyson won a $500 prize.

Wilson, who in 2009 was inducted into the Pro Football Hall of Fame in Canton, Ohio, is the only original AFL owner to keep his team in its originating city. He played a major role in the AFL-NFL merger, known as "the voice of reason" among the owners.

Wilson's Bills also won two AFL titles in 1964 and '65, were the only AFL team to reach the postseason in four consecutive years (1963-66), and were alone in winning four straight AFC titles (1990-93) to be first to appear in four straight Super Bowls.

The *Buffalo News* named Wilson, who is age 92 at this writing, the Buffalo area's top sports figure in the past millennium.

QUESTION 1: Who was the Bills coach who led them to two league championships in the 1960s?
- a) Buster Ramsey
- b) Chuck Knox
- c) Lou Saban
- d) Jim Ringo

QUESTION 2: Who was the Bills' first draft choice in their first American Football League season of 1960?
- a) Richie Lucas, quarterback, Penn State
- b) Stew Barber, tackle, Penn State
- c) Billy Shaw, tackle, Georgia Tech
- d) Willie Evans, running back, Buffalo

QUESTION 3: What was the most popular nickname given to the Bills' first home of War Memorial Stadium?
- a) The Monument to Decay
- b) The Rockpile
- c) The House That Ralph Built
- d) Rich Stadium

QUESTION 4: Who was the Bills' first general manager?
- a) Truman Bledsoe
- b) Drew Bledsoe
- c) Bill Polian
- d) Dick Gallagher

QUESTION 5: In the early years of the franchise, who was known as "Golden Wheels?"
- a) Cookie Gilchrist
- b) Elbert Dubenion
- c) J.D. Hill
- d) Butch Byrd

QUESTION 6: How did the Bills get their name?

a) Owner Ralph Wilson selected it
b) A fan, James Dyson, suggested it back in the All-America Conference team's era in 1946
c) The Buffalo Chamber of Commerce picked it
d) Eventual longtime radio play-caller Van Miller drew the winning name from a hat

QUESTION 7: When did the Bills play an NFL opponent for the first time and which team was it?
a) In 1966 against the Pittsburgh Steelers
b) In a 1967 preseason game, losing to the Lions in Detroit
c) They upset the San Francisco 49ers in 1972
d) They lost to the Washington Redskins in a 1973 preseason game

QUESTION 8: Which veteran writer covered the Bills for two Buffalo daily newspapers?
a) Larry Felser
b) Jim Peters
c) Jim Baker
d) Milt Northrop

QUESTION 9: Where was the Bills' first training camp?
a) Niagara University
b) Behind a motor hotel in Hamburg, N.Y.
c) Behind the Roycroft Inn, East Aurora
d) State University of NY at Fredonia

QUESTION 10: How did the Patriots hold O.J. Simpson to only eight yards in a 1972 game in New England?
a) He was injured before halftime
b) He was late arriving due to a domestic abuse incident
c) He was ejected for fighting
d) He and good buddy Al Cowlings were detained at the hotel for trashing their room

QUESTION 11: The only NFL game ever played in San Antonio featured the Bills and New Orleans Saints. Why was it played there?
- a) The Saints were considering a move to New Orleans
- b) The Saints were displaced due to Hurricane Katrina and San Antonio became the alternate site
- c) Because of a flu epidemic, the game site had to be switched
- d) The Bills' plane had an extreme weather problem, was diverted to San Antonio one day before the game and the NFL decided to play it there

QUESTION 12: Who was the Bills' most successful quarterback?
- a) Jim Kelly
- b) Jack Kemp
- c) Daryle Lamonica
- d) Joe Ferguson

QUESTION 13: Who enjoyed the longest tenure of any Bills' coach?
- a) Lou Saban
- b) Marv Levy
- c) Harvey Johnson
- d) Joel Collier

QUESTION 14: Which Bills' player became more famous off the field before O.J. Simpson was charged with murdering his wife, Nicole?
- a) Jack Kemp
- b) Cookie Gilchrist
- c) Paul Maguire
- d) Tom Sestak

QUESTION 15: How many victories did five-time Bills' Pro Bowl nose tackle Fred Smerlas have during his senior season at Boston College?

a) 10
b) 12
c) 4
d) 0

QUESTION 16: Who engineered the Bills' stirring comeback from a 35-3 deficit to topple Houston in the infamous January 3, 1993, AFC Wild Card game—the greatest comeback in NFL history?
a) Jim Kelly
b) Joe Ferguson
c) Frank Reich
d) Dennis Shaw

QUESTION 17: How long was Scott Norwood's wide field goal attempt on the last play that kept the Bills from winning their first Super Bowl in a stinging 20-19 defeat to the New York Giants on January 27, 1991?
a) 52 yards
b) 47 yards
c) 55 yards
d) 35 yards

QUESTION 18: Who nailed San Diego running back Keith Lincoln with "The Hit Heard Around the World," breaking one of his ribs in stirring the Bills to their first AFL title, 20-7, on December 20, 1964?
a) Robert James
b) Mike Stratton
c) Tom Sestak
d) Ron McDole

QUESTION 19: Who starred as the heavy-underdog Bills stunned the Chargers in San Diego, 23-0, on December 26, 1965, to capture their second straight AFL crown?
a) Pete Gogolak
b) Jack Kemp

c) Ernie Warlick

d) Butch Byrd

QUESTION 20: Who fumbled inside the Oakland one-yard line, preserving a 13-10 Raiders' win in the 1968 season's semifinal game, eventually allowing the Bills to take O.J. Simpson with the NFL's top 1969 draft choice?

a) Jack Kemp

b) Ed Rutkowski

c) Max Anderson

d) Gary McDermott

QUESTION 21: What Bills' coach decided to use O.J. Simpson as a virtual decoy through much of his first Buffalo season despite having won the Heisman Trophy with Southern Cal?

a) Lou Saban

b) Harvey Johnson

c) Joe Collier

d) John Rauch

QUESTION 22: O.J.'s No. 32 became famous to fans and foes, but what was his first number with the Bills?

a) 24

b) 32

c) 36

d) 30

QUESTION 23: Why was Buffalo's offensive line that blocked so well in 1973 nicknamed the Electric Company?

a) O.J.'s rushing yardage was so shocking after his pro career's slow start

b) It turned loose the Juice—who rolled up an NFL record 2,003 rushing yards that season

c) Because O.J. had so many electrifying runs

d) Because that rushing attack sparked the once-lethargic Bills into the playoffs

QUESTION 24: Though the Bills drafted Jim Kelly in 1983, he did not play with hem until 1986. Why not?
   a) He stayed in college
   b) He was playing in the USFL
   c) He was a contractual holdout
   d) He wanted to play for his hometown of Pittsburgh

QUESTION 25: What poetic expression did Reggie McKenzie use to celebrate O.J.'s dominance of the Patriots?
   a) Nothing could be finer than to lay a block on (Steve) Kiner!
   b) I can sound like a bard 'cause they can't handle a pulling guard!
   c) When we play the Pats, he'll run, run, run for fun, fun, fun!
   d) To loosen the Pats, it's the Juice who's loose!

Chapter One Answer Key

___ **Question 1:** C   ___ **Question 14:** A
___ **Question 2:** A   ___ **Question 15:** D
___ **Question 3:** B   ___ **Question 16:** C
___ **Question 4:** D   ___ **Question 17:** B
___ **Question 5:** B   ___ **Question 18:** B
___ **Question 6:** A & B   ___ **Question 19:** A
___ **Question 7:** B   ___ **Question 20:** B
___ **Question 8:** A   ___ **Question 21:** D
___ **Question 9:** C   ___ **Question 22:** C
___ **Question 10:** C   ___ **Question 23:** B
___ **Question 11:** B   ___ **Question 24:** B
___ **Question 12:** A   ___ **Question 25:** A
___ **Question 13:** B

Keep a running tally of your correct answers!

Number correct: __ / 25

Overall correct: __ / 25

"You know the reason I'm here. I don't need to play the game for any other reason than to win a championship!"
— *Drew Bledsoe*

Chapter Two

Drew Bledsoe

DREW BLEDSOE STARRED as the New England Patriots' strong-armed quarterback and that franchise's leading passer in a glowing nine-year career until injured in a controversial sideline play against the New York Jets in 2001. He was idle most of that season in favor of Tom Brady, but returned to throw a TD pass to lead the Pats' victory over Pittsburgh in the AFC title game.

He was traded in 2002 to the Bills for their top 2003 draft choice.

Bledsoe lost little time in making a strong impact, starting all 16 games in 2002 and setting ten franchise records. They included single-season marks for passing yards, attempts, completions and 300-yard games. He made the Pro Bowl for a fourth time that year and his two overtime game-winning passes gave him four for a career, most of any quarterback in NFL history.

QUESTION 26: Who holds the Bills and NFL record for the most receiving yards in a postseason game?
  a) Eric Moulds
  b) Frank Lewis
  c) Andre Reed
  d) James Lofton

QUESTION 27: Why did Bills' equipment manager Tony Marchitte have a hard time finding a helmet for O.J.?
  a) The NFL's top 1969 draft choice required a specially equipped helmet to protect him
  b) His head was too large—literally
  c) O.J. objected to the standing-buffalo decal and insisted on a running buffalo
  d) O.J. wanted the same interior style worn by good friend Al Cowlings

QUESTION 28: Who couldn't go in snow when the Bills played the Patriots in a playoff game at Fenway Park?
   a) O.J. Simpson
   b) Jim Braxton
   c) Billy Joe
   d) Cookie Gilchrist

QUESTION 29: Who became the sixth head coach in the Bills' history after Lou Saban suddenly resigned in 1976?
   a) Harvey Johnson
   b) Chuck Knox
   c) Joe Collier
   d) Jim Ringo

QUESTION 30: What was the Bills' present home originally called?
   a) Orchard Park Stadium
   b) Erie County Stadium
   c) Rich Stadium
   d) Ralph Wilson Stadium

QUESTION 31: Buffalo's favorite football team is the Bills, but what is Western New York's favorite food?
   a) Cheeseburger
   b) Hot Dog
   c) Chicken Wings
   d) Tacos

QUESTION 32: Who was the Bills' starting quarterback immediately before Joe Ferguson?
   a) Gary Marangi
   b) Dennis Shaw
   c) Ed Rutkowski
   d) Jack Kemp

QUESTION 33: What former Bills' official was the University of Miami's athletic director when Jim Kelly starred there?

a) Lou Saban
b) Bill Polian
c) Chuck Knox
d) Earthquake Enyart

QUESTION 34: What former Bills' player visited O.J. Simpson in jail and died shortly thereafter?
a) Jim Braxton
b) John Leypoldt
c) Bob Chandler
d) Edgar Chandler

QUESTION 35: Who caught Jim Kelly's first Bills' touchdown pass?
a) Andre Reed
b) Thurman Thomas
c) James Lofton
d) Greg Bell

QUESTION 36: Who switched playing positions most dramatically during the Lou Saban era?
a) Dwight Harrison
b) Paul Seymour
c) Paul Guidry
d) Jim Cheyunski

QUESTION 37: Who were the main players the Bills received from Oakland for quarterback Daryle Lamonica and wide receiver Glenn Bass in what's generally regarded as their worst trade ever?
a) Quarterback Tom Flores and wide receiver Art Powell
b) Middle linebacker Jim Cheyunski and center Mike Montler
c) Linebacker Tom Cousineau and running back Wayne Patrick
d) Two draft choices

QUESTION 38: What popular musicians entertained Bills' fans during games in the early years at War Memorial Stadium?

    a) Guy Lombardo and his Royal Canadians

    b) Eli Konikoff and his Dixieland Six

    c) The Spike Jones Band

    d) The Buffalo Bills quartet

QUESTION 39: What Bills second-round draft choice played on the AFL title teams of 1964 and '65, was an All-AFL first team pick from 1962-66, second team choice in 1968 and '69, made the all-time All-AFL team, and in 1999 became the second former Bill (after O.J.) named to the Pro Football Hall of Fame?

    a) Jack Kemp

    b) Jim Dunaway

    c) Paul Maguire

    d) Billy Shaw

QUESTION 40: What Bills' coach known for malapropos blamed the media for a mid-1980s defeat, claiming it "knocked the sails out of our wind?"

    a) John Rauch

    b) Hank Bullough

    c) Harvey Johnson

    d) Kay Stephenson

QUESTION 41: What was Tom Day's nickname?

    a) Tippy

    b) Tipsy

    c) Crash

    d) Wild Thing

QUESTION 42: What was Eddie Abramoski's title with the Bills from the team's inception in 1960 to 1995?

    a) Ralph Wilson's Driver

    b) Public Relations Director

    c) Operations Director

    d) Trainer

QUESTION 43: What Bills' teammates opened a popular restaurant-bar in suburban Cheektowaga?
   a) Billy Shaw and Jim Dunaway
   b) Paul Guidry and Edgar Chandler
   c) Tom Sestak and Paul Maguire
   d) Earl Campbell

QUESTION 44: Who kicked the longest field goal in Bills' history and what was the distance?
   a) Scott Norwood, 50
   b) John Leypoldt, 51
   c) Steve Christie, 59
   d) Pete Gogolak, 49

QUESTION 45: Who made the longest run from scrimmage in Bills' history and how long was it?
   a) Greg Bell, 85 vs. Dallas (1984)
   b) O.J. Simpson, 94 vs. Pittsburgh (1972)
   c) Wray Carlton, 80 vs. Houston (1965)
   d) Thurman Thomas, 80 vs. New England (1990)

QUESTION 46: Who scored the most Bills' touchdowns in one game (five)?
   a) O.J. Simpson
   b) Cookie Gilchrist
   c) Jerry Butler
   d) Roland Hooks

QUESTION 47: Who played the most regular-season games in a Bills' career?
   a) Bruce Smith
   b) Jim Kelly
   c) Joe Devlin
   d) Andre Reed

QUESTION 48: How many Bills' head coaches have there been through 2010?

a) 16
b) 14
c) 17
d) 20

QUESTION 49: In what year did O.J. Simpson break the NFL single-season rushing record?
a) 1972
b) 1973
c) 1974
d) 1978

QUESTION 50: Who was the first Bills' player to have his uniform number retired?
a) O.J. Simpson
b) Cookie Gilchrist
c) Jim Kelly
d) Jack Kemp

CHAPTER TWO ANSWER KEY

___ **QUESTION 26:** A
___ **QUESTION 27:** B
___ **QUESTION 28:** D
___ **QUESTION 29:** D
___ **QUESTION 30:** C
___ **QUESTION 31:** C
___ **QUESTION 32:** B
___ **QUESTION 33:** A
___ **QUESTION 34:** C
___ **QUESTION 35:** D
___ **QUESTION 36:** A
___ **QUESTION 37:** A
___ **QUESTION 38:** B

___ **QUESTION 39:** D
___ **QUESTION 40:** B
___ **QUESTION 41:** A
___ **QUESTION 42:** D
___ **QUESTION 43:** C
___ **QUESTION 44:** C
___ **QUESTION 45:** B
___ **QUESTION 46:** B
___ **QUESTION 47:** D
___ **QUESTION 48:** A
___ **QUESTION 49:** B
___ **QUESTION 50:** C

KEEP A RUNNING TALLY OF YOUR CORRECT ANSWERS!

Number correct: ___ / 25

Overall correct: ___ / 50

"Without O.J. my rookie year could have been a nightmare. He helped me in so many ways. He had such a great year, that took the pressure right away from me. Because of him, I was able to come along slowly. The other teams' linebackers, for example, had to honor his play fakes and that kept them off me."
— Joe Ferguson

Chapter Three

Joe Ferguson

I WAS COVERING the Bills for *The Buffalo Courier-Express* in 1973 when I spotted the broad smile on Coach Lou Saban's face as he guided Joe Ferguson in the early days of training camp. Saban had enough of previous starter Dennis Shaw's inconsistencies and that's why the Bills made Ferguson their first of two third-round '73 draft choices. His passes were crisp and he showed good field general skills, especially for a rookie.

He was to be the Bills' starting quarterback for most of O.J. Simpson's era in Buffalo.

In fact, Ferguson quarterbacked the Bills from 1973-84 and led them in passing all 12 of those seasons. He set virtually every Bills passing mark during the '70s and early '80s.

On October 9, 1983, the first-year Arkansas rifle set the Bills' single-game mark in pass attempts (55), completions (35) and aerial yards (419) in throwing for five touchdowns as the Bills ended years of frustration against Miami with a 38-35 overtime victory. He ranks second in team history in career pass attempts (4,166), completions (2,188), aerial yards (27,590) and touchdowns (181).

Ferguson had a hangdog look after interceptions, but the fact is he did far more than hand off to Simpson during their tremendous success together.

QUESTION 51: When was the Bills Wall of Fame created?
 a) 1980
 b) 1985
 c) 1972
 d) 1990

QUESTION 52: How many times during Jim Kelly's 11 seasons with the Bills did he pass for more than 300 yards in a game?
 a) 20
 b) 25

c) 26

d) 18

QUESTION 53: For how many years had Marv Levy been a coach before he came to the Bills in 1987?

a) 20

b) 25

c) 15

d) More than 30

QUESTION 54: How did the Bills obtain quarterback Drew Bledsoe?

a) By trade for New England's No. 1 draft choice in 2003

b) By trade for New England's No. 1 draft choice in 2004

c) Signed as free agent

d) He was their top draft choice in 2002

QUESTION 55: Who was the Bills' top draft choice in 1996?

a) Eric Moulds

b) Traded to Jacksonville for quarterback Rob Johnson

c) Ruben Brown

d) Travis Henry

QUESTION 56: What was the Bills' longest single-game pass connection of 98 yards and a touchdown?

a) Doug Flutie to Eric Moulds in 1998

b) Jack Kemp to Glenn Bass in 1964

c) Jack Kemp to Elbert Dubenion in 1963

d) Ryan Fitzpatrick to Terrell Owens in 2009

QUESTION 57: Who threw the most Bills' interceptions (26) in a single season?

a) Jack Kemp

b) Joe Ferguson

c) Dennis Shaw

d) Jim Kelly

QUESTION 58: Who threw the most passing touchdowns in a Bills' game, season and career?
a) Joe Ferguson
b) Jack Kemp
c) Jim Kelly
d) Drew Bledsoe

QUESTION 59: Who holds the Bills' record for the most career aerial receiving yards?
a) Andre Reed
b) Elbert Dubenion
c) Jerry Butler
d) Bob Chandler

QUESTION 60: What defensive back holds the Bills' record of 40 career interceptions?
a) Tony Greene
b) Butch Byrd
c) Booker Edgerson
d) Steve Freeman

QUESTION 61: Who has been the most honored of Bills' offensive linemen?
a) Reggie McKenzie
b) Joe DeLamielleure
c) Billy Shaw
d) Kent Hull

QUESTION 62: What Bills' defensive lineman made the most quarterback sacks in NFL history?
a) Tom Sestak
b) Ron McDole
c) Bruce Smith
d) Cornelius Bennett

QUESTION 63: Who recovered the most fumbles in a Bills' career?

    a) Bruce Smith
    b) Cornelius Bennett
    c) Jim Dunaway
    d) Tony Greene

QUESTION 64: Who has made the Bills' longest punt return of 91 yards?
    a) Hagood Clarke
    b) Ed Rutkowski
    c) Keith Moody
    d) Butch Byrd

QUESTION 65: What Bills' receiver was the first NFL player to score a touchdown in the 1970s, 1980s, and 1990s?
    a) Andre Reed
    b) Jerry Butler
    c) Frank Lewis
    d) James Lofton

QUESTION 66: Who attempted the most rushes and gained the most ground yardage in a Bills' career?
    a) Thurman Thomas
    b) Joe Cribbs
    c) O.J. Simpson
    d) Cookie Gilchrist

QUESTION 67: Who has the Bills' highest punting average for one season and a career?
    a) Marv Bateman
    b) Paul Maguire
    c) Billy Atkins
    d) John Kidd

QUESTION 68: How many Bills are in the Pro Football Hall of Fame?
    a) 3
    b) 4

c) 5

d) 2

QUESTION 69: What team dashed the Bills' 1974 title hopes?
a) Cleveland
b) Kansas City
c) Pittsburgh
d) San Diego

QUESTION 70: What team ended the Bills' quest for a third straight AFL title and prevented them from making the first Super Bowl?
a) Kansas City
b) New York Jets
c) San Diego
d) Boston Patriots

QUESTION 71: Why did an out-of-town hotel clerk tell team owner Ralph Wilson that the Bills had not yet arrived?
a) Wilson went to the wrong hotel
b) The clerk had only heard of the Bills' barbershop quartet, not the football team
c) The game date was changed at the last minute
d) The clerk was playing a practical joke

QUESTION 72: Where was O.J. Simpson's since-eclipsed NFL rushing record set in 1973?
a) Detroit
b) New York
c) Orchard Park
d) Buffalo

QUESTION 73: In 2008, the Bills became the first NFL team to host a regular season game in Canada. How many games will they play in Toronto?

a) The Toronto series calls for one regular season game in
   2011 and 2012 plus a preseason game in 2012
b) Eight more through 2014
c) Nine more through 2015
d) Ten more through 2020

QUESTION 74: How did the Bills acquire quarterback Ryan
Fitzpatrick?
a) Trade with Cincinnati
b) Seventh-round draft choice
c) Free agent
d) Trade with St. Louis

QUESTION 75: How many training camp sites have the Bills
had?
a) 4
b) 6
c) 3
d) 5

CHAPTER THREE ANSWER KEY

___ **QUESTION 51:** A
___ **QUESTION 52:** C
___ **QUESTION 53:** D
___ **QUESTION 54:** A
___ **QUESTION 55:** A
___ **QUESTION 56:** D
___ **QUESTION 57:** A & C
___ **QUESTION 58:** C
___ **QUESTION 59:** A
___ **QUESTION 60:** B
___ **QUESTION 61:** B
___ **QUESTION 62:** C
___ **QUESTION 63:** B

___ **QUESTION 64:** C
___ **QUESTION 65:** D
___ **QUESTION 66:** A
___ **QUESTION 67:** B
___ **QUESTION 68:** C
___ **QUESTION 69:** C
___ **QUESTION 70:** A
___ **QUESTION 71:** B
___ **QUESTION 72:** B
___ **QUESTION 73:** A
___ **QUESTION 74:** C
___ **QUESTION 75:** D

KEEP A RUNNING TALLY OF YOUR CORRECT ANSWERS!

Number correct: ___ / 25

Overall correct: ___ / 75

"This is my hobby."
— Doug Flutie

Chapter Four

Doug Flutie

DOUG FLUTIE'S CAREER at Boston College is best known for his 48-yard desperate last-play touchdown heave to Gerard Phelan that lifted the Eagles to a miraculous 47-45 triumph over the University of Miami at the Orange Bowl in 1984. The diminutive (5-feet-9) quarterback was already a lock for the Heisman Trophy before that nationally televised drama in which Flutie outdueled the Hurricanes' Bernie Kosar.

But Flutie had plenty of drama left for his Bills' career after becoming the team's quarterback five games into the 1998 season.

His reputation as a miracle worker continued as he replaced injured Rob Johnson and threw two TD passes in a fourth-quarter comeback that beat the Indianapolis Colts. The following week, in his first NFL start since 1989, his fourth-down bootleg in the waning seconds upended previously unbeaten Jacksonville.

Flutie's record as a 1998 starter was 8-3, but tough luck was to follow. First, his fumble on the five-yard line with 17 seconds left cost a first-round playoff loss to Miami. Then, after leading the Bills to a 10-5 record in '99, coach Wade Phillips replaced him as the starter against eventual AFC champion Tennessee. That game became known for the "Music City Miracle" when the Bills' apparent winning field goal was followed by a wild game-winning kickoff return. After the 22-16 Bills defeat, Phillips said he was ordered by Bills owner Ralph Wilson to replace Flutie with Johnson.

As this is written, the Bills have not appeared in a playoff game since and that fact is known as the "Flutie Curse." Yet Flutie, a Canadian League Hall of Famer, found some measure of revenge in 2001 when he signed with San Diego and broke a sack attempt to dash 13 yards for a game-winning TD that defeated Johnson and the Bills.

QUESTION 76: When was the Bills' home stadium in Orchard Park, initially called Rich Stadium and now Ralph Wilson Stadium, completed?

    a)   1972
    b)   1973
    c)   1974
    d)   1975

QUESTION 77: Who won the first game ever played in the Orchard Park stadium?

    a)   Washington
    b)   Bills
    c)   New England
    d)   Miami

QUESTION 78: What is the largest paid crowd to see a Bills' home game?

    a)   80,020
    b)   80,368
    c)   80,243
    d)   78,548

QUESTION 79: Who is the Bills' career scoring leader?

    a)   Andre Reed
    b)   Thurman Thomas
    c)   O.J. Simpson
    d)   Steve Christie

QUESTION 80: Who scored the most Bills' points in a single season?

    a)   O.J. Simpson
    b)   Cookie Gilchrist
    c)   Scott Norwood
    d)   Steve Christie

QUESTION 81: What Bills record was broken with a resounding 17-7 home victory in 1980?
- a) The Bills had lost 20 straight games to Miami before winning this one
- b) Fewest penalty yards in a game
- c) Most penalty yards in a game
- d) Fewest turnovers in a game

QUESTION 82: Who holds the Bills' record for single-season passing attempts, yards gained and completions?
- a) Jim Kelly
- b) Joe Ferguson
- c) Drew Bledsoe
- d) Jack Kemp

QUESTION 83: Who holds the Bills' record for most rushing yards in a game (273)?
- a) O.J. Simpson
- b) Cookie Gilchrist
- c) Thurman Thomas
- d) Terry Miller

QUESTION 84: Who holds the Bills' record for most games rushing for 200-plus yards in a season?
- a) Thurman Thomas
- b) O.J. Simpson
- c) Cookie Gilchrist
- d) Greg Bell

QUESTION 85: Who holds the Bills' record for most 200-plus-yard games in a career?
- a) O.J. Simpson
- b) Thurman Thomas
- c) Cookie Gilchrist
- d) Wray Carlton

QUESTION 86: Who holds the Bills' record for most career kickoff returns (101)?
 a) Charley Warner
 b) Keith Moody
 c) Eric Moulds
 d) Kevin Williams

QUESTION 87: Who holds the Bills' record for most career punt returns (100)?
 a) Keith Moody
 b) Butch Byrd
 c) Donnie Walker
 d) Jeff Burris

QUESTION 88: Who holds the Bills' career PATs record (309)?
 a) Scott Norwood
 b) John Leypoldt
 c) Steve Christie
 d) Booth Lusteg

QUESTION 89: Who holds the Bills' record for most PATs in a single season (56)?
 a) Steve Christie
 b) Scott Norwood
 c) John Leypoldt
 d) Booth Lusteg

QUESTION 90: Who holds the Bills' single-game PAT record?
 a) Booth Lusteg
 b) Scott Norwood
 c) John Leypoldt
 d) Steve Christie

QUESTION 91: Which team did the Bills defeat for their first regular season victory?
 a) New York Titans
 b) Boston Patriots

c) Denver Broncos
d) Kansas City Chiefs

QUESTION 92: Who was the Bills' original radio voice?
a) Al Meltzer
b) John Murphy
c) Van Miller
d) Stan Barron

QUESTION 93: Who was Miller's longstanding radio partner who succeeded him on play-by-play?
a) John Murphy
b) Ed Kilgore
c) Rick Azar
d) Clip Smith

QUESTION 94: Who is the popular Western New York product that frequently calls Bills' telecasts on CBS?
a) Jim Nantz
b) Joe Buck
c) Al Michaels
d) Don Criqui

QUESTION 95: How many years had Van Miller called Bills' radio broadcasts when he retired in 2003?
a) 20
b) 35
c) 37
d) 50

QUESTION 96: In what year did the Bills bid farewell via salary cap moves to three of the franchise's greatest players—Bruce Smith, Andre Reed and Thurman Thomas?
a) 1999
b) 2000
c) 2001
d) 2002

QUESTION 97: Who was the Bills' quarterback when they lost a 1999 Wild Card playoff game to Tennessee via a controversial trick play for a decisive touchdown after a field goal gave the Bills seeming victory?
   a) Doug Flutie
   b) Rob Johnson
   c) Jim Kelly
   d) Todd Collins

QUESTION 98: Before the Bills' stadium became named after owner Ralph Wilson, it carried what name dating to 1973?
   a) Orchard Park Stadium
   b) Erie County Stadium
   c) Bills Park
   d) Rich Stadium

QUESTION 99: What is the Bills' most noted accomplishment in the team's history?
   a) Winning four consecutive AFC titles to become the only team in NFL history to reach four straight Super Bowls
   b) Winning back-to-back AFL titles in 1964 and '65
   c) Having a quarterback (Jim Kelly) and running back (O.J. Simpson) who shattered NFL passing and rushing marks in different eras
   d) Having home attendances that repeatedly led pro football

QUESTION 100: The Bills lost four straight Super Bowls from 1991-95, but which was the only team to defeat them twice in the NFL's showcase game?
   a) New York Giants
   b) Dallas Cowboys
   c) Washington Redskins
   d) Philadelphia Eagles

CHAPTER FOUR ANSWER KEY

___ **QUESTION 76**: B   ___ **QUESTION 89**: B
___ **QUESTION 77**: A   ___ **QUESTION 90**: A
___ **QUESTION 78**: B   ___ **QUESTION 91**: B
___ **QUESTION 79**: D   ___ **QUESTION 92**: C
___ **QUESTION 80**: D   ___ **QUESTION 93**: A
___ **QUESTION 81**: A   ___ **QUESTION 94**: D
___ **QUESTION 82**: C   ___ **QUESTION 95**: C
___ **QUESTION 83**: A   ___ **QUESTION 96**: B
___ **QUESTION 84**: B   ___ **QUESTION 97**: B
___ **QUESTION 85**: A   ___ **QUESTION 98**: D
___ **QUESTION 86**: B   ___ **QUESTION 99**: A
___ **QUESTION 87**: D   ___ **QUESTION 100**: B
___ **QUESTION 88**: C

KEEP A RUNNING TALLY OF YOUR CORRECT ANSWERS!

Number correct: ___ / 25

Overall correct: ___ / 100

"Pro football gave me a good perspective. When I entered the political arena, I had already been booed, cheered, cut, sold, traded, and hung in effigy."
— Jack Kemp

Chapter Five

Jack Kemp

IT CERTAINLY DIDN'T take Jack Kemp long to find his niche as the Bills' starting quarterback after coming to the team for the incredibly low waiver price of $100 from San Diego in 1962. He was a scrambler at first and later an outstanding pocket quarterback—though only six feet tall—with an occasional affinity for gambling plays. He and coach Lou Saban formed an outstanding combination in the AFL's early years, leading the Bills to consecutive league championships in 1964 and '65.

Kemp also had an intra-squad rivalry with Daryle Lamonica, a more flashy sort, and the two triggered debates among Bills' fans of who was the better quarterback—a steady Kemp or the mad-bomber Lamonica, the former Notre Dame star who arrived as Buffalo's 24th pick of the 1963 draft.

Kemp was the starter, but Bills fans loved it when Lamonica came off the bench to inject life into the offense, often via long passes. Kemp-Lamonica debates raged until 1967, when Lamonica was traded to Oakland with wide receiver Glenn Bass for quarterback Tom Flores and wide receiver Art Powell plus draft choices both ways.

The trade is generally regarded the worst in Bills' history. Lamonica became a standout in leading a tremendous Raiders team while Flores and Powell disappointed with the Bills. Still, Kemp and Lamonica keyed the Bills' title teams of 1964 and '65 plus the Eastern Division winners of '66 that lost the AFL title game to Kansas City, which went on to the first-ever Super Bowl.

Kemp's 42-yard pass to Bass set up Kemp's one-yard TD sneak that finished the scoring in the Bills' 20-7 victory over the Chargers, Kemp's former team, in the 1964 title game. That same game featured such a jarring tackle by Mike Stratton that Chargers' star running back Keith Lincoln was forced from the game with a broken rib. "The Hit Heard Around the World" changed momentum after San Diego scored early. Kemp was steady, but Bills fullback Cookie Gilchrist starred with 122 rushing yards.

A year later in San Diego, the Chargers were heavily favored in the title rematch, but the Bills prevailed, 23-0, behind staunch defense and Kemp, who was voted MVP.

Kemp hit tight end Ernie Warlick for the game's first TD before Butch Byrd's 74-yard punt return produced another score. The Buffalo defense completely thwarted San Diego's usually explosive offense and Pete Gogolak booted three field goals from 11, 39 and 32 yards.

Kemp connected with Elbert Dubenion on a 69-yard game-tying TD bomb in the next AFL title game, but had two interceptions as Len Dawson led Kansas City past the Bills, 31-7, to reach the first Super Bowl against Green Bay.

Kemp's last season was O.J. Simpson's first with the Bills in 1969.

Kemp was noted on Buffalo road trips for frequently reading historical and political books during charter flights and after his retirement he became a popular U.S. representative from the Buffalo area. He grew increasingly involved in governmental affairs, was an outspoken Congressman and in 1996 was the Vice-Presidential candidate as Senator Robert Dole's running mate against Bill Clinton and Al Gore.

Kemp's eight-year Bills statistics: 1,040 completions, 2,240 pass attempts, 15,138 yards, 77 touchdowns, and 132 interceptions in 88 games. He compiled a 46.4 completion percentage.

He died at age 75 on May 2, 2009—barely a month after Saban passed away at age 87 on March 29.

QUESTION 101: What Bills punter placed the most punts inside opponents' 20-yard line?
   a) Paul Maguire
   b) John Kidd
   c) Chris Mohr
   d) Brian Moorman

QUESTION 102: What national TV commentator regularly says: "No team circles the wagons like the Buffalo Bills"?
a) John Madden
b) Phil Simms
c) Chris Berman
d) Al Michaels

QUESTION 103: Who was the Bills' popular public relations director when O.J. Simpson joined the team in 1972?
a) L. Budd Thalman
b) Jack Horrigan
c) Scott Berchtold
d) Chuck Burr

QUESTION 104: Besides the spectacular comeback from 32 points behind to topple Houston in the 1993 AFC Wild Card game, what was the Bills' next greatest comeback?
a) Antowain Smith led a powerful rally from a 26-0 deficit to nip Indianapolis, 37-35, in 1997
b) Scott Norwood's 27-yard overtime field goal capped a surge from 21 points down to beat Miami, 34-31, in 1987
c) Rallying from 19-0 to beat Minnesota, 23-22, in 1982
d) Edging Carolina, 25-24, after trailing by 24-6 in 2001

QUESTION 105: What cornerback rose from being an undrafted 1969 free agent to record nine career interceptions and make three straight Pro Bowls?
a) Butch Byrd
b) Booker Edgerson
c) Robert James
d) Tony Greene

QUESTION 106: After O.J. Simpson asked for a trade, then was wooed back for a $2.5 million deal before the 1976 opener, who confronted owner Ralph Wilson during a practice and wanted to renegotiate?

a) Jim Braxton
b) Joe Ferguson
c) Ahmad Rashad
d) J.D. Hill

QUESTION 107: What Bills' head coach also coached in the World Football League?
a) Lou Saban
b) Chan Gailey
c) Chuck Knox
d) Kay Stephenson

QUESTION 108: Who led the Bills in passing for 12 consecutive seasons?
a) Jim Kelly
b) Jack Kemp
c) Dennis Shaw
d) Joe Ferguson

QUESTION 109: Who kicked the most consecutive Bills' field goals (18)?
a) John Leypoldt
b) Steve Christie
c) Rian Lindell
d) Booth Lusteg

QUESTION 110: Who is credited with forcing the most safeties in a Bills' season and career?
a) Mike Stratton
b) Tom Sestak
c) Bruce Smith
d) Ron McDole

QUESTION 111: Who coached the most Bills games (182) and won the most in a career (112) and single season (13)?
a) Lou Saban
b) Chuck Knox

c) Marv Levy
d) Hank Bullough

QUESTION 112: Who quarterbacked the All-America Conference Bills, then when that team folded joined the Cleveland Browns?
a) Lou Saban
b) Otto Graham
c) George Ratterman
d) Y.A. Tittle

QUESTION 113: Who threw the most Bills' interceptions in a game (6) and career (190)?
a) Joe Ferguson
b) Jack Kemp
c) Jim Kelly
d) Rob Johnson

QUESTION 114: Who among ABC's Monday Night Football announcers was most influential in O.J. Simpson joining them?
a) Keith Jackson
b) Howard Cosell
c) Frank Gifford
d) Don Meredith

QUESTION 115: How did the Bills acquire controversial wide receiver Terrell Owens in 2009?
a) Trade with Dallas
b) He was a free agent after Dallas released him
c) Trade with Cincinnati
d) Trade with Philadelphia

QUESTION 116: In 1965, the Bills set a record with the most players participating in the AFL All-Star Game. How many Bills participated?
a) 10
b) 12

c) 20
d) The entire Bills 40-man team played the AFL All-Stars

QUESTION 117: During the second Lou Saban era, the coach would occasionally look up suspiciously at a helicopter hovering over his practice. Who did he suspect was spying on the Bills?
a) Oakland Raiders' boss Al Davis
b) The NFL office
c) Miami Dolphins coach Don Shula
d) One AFC East coach after another

QUESTION 118: What is "The Foolish Club"?
a) A group of early AFL owners who made foolish wagers on their teams' success
b) Bills' founder and only president Ralph C. Wilson Jr. joined his fellow original AFL owners in this club, so named for the appearance that their investments in founding a second pro football league were foolish
c) The name affixed to newspaper prognosticators who saw the AFL beating the NFL in early Super Bowls
d) The name given to those who predicted Joe Namath's NY Jets would upset Baltimore in Super Bowl III

QUESTION 119: Who was Charlie (Slivers) Ferguson?
a) A little-known Bills' wide receiver of 1969 until he snared a winning touchdown bomb from Jack Kemp— moving *Courier-Express* columnist Phil Ranallo to dub him "Slivers" for all the time he spent on the bench
b) A distant relative of quarterback Joe Ferguson
c) The Bills' first free agent roster addition
d) A Bills' "super fan" of their four-Super Bowl era

QUESTION 120: Who was the Bills' general manager who built the team that went to four straight Super Bowls?
a) Hank Bullough
b) Dick Gallagher

c) John Butler
d) Marv Levy

QUESTION 121: How did linebacker Tom Cousineau figure in Jim Kelly's Bills' arrival?
a) Kelly was traded from Cleveland for Cousineau in a straight player deal
b) Kelly was traded from his native Pittsburgh in exchange for rights to Cousineau
c) Cousineau exited via free agency as Kelly arrived
d) Kelly was selected with the 1982 first-round draft choice obtained from Cleveland in the trade for Cousineau

QUESTION 122: Which Bills' coach played for the Cleveland Browns?
a) Chuck Knox
b) Lou Saban
c) Chan Gailey
d) Joe Collier

QUESTION 123: How many 13-victory regular seasons have the Bills posted?
a) One
b) Two
c) Three
d) Four

QUESTION 124: How many Bills' uniform numbers have been retired?
a) One—Jim Kelly
b) Two—Kelly and O.J. Simpson
c) Three—Kelly, O.J. and Jack Kemp
d) None

QUESTION 125: In what round of the 1972 draft did the Bills select Reggie McKenzie?

a) Second
b) Third
c) First
d) Fifth

CHAPTER FIVE ANSWER KEY

___ **QUESTION 101:** D
___ **QUESTION 102:** C
___ **QUESTION 103:** B
___ **QUESTION 104:** A
___ **QUESTION 105:** C
___ **QUESTION 106:** A
___ **QUESTION 107:** B
___ **QUESTION 108:** D
___ **QUESTION 109:** C
___ **QUESTION 110:** D
___ **QUESTION 111:** C
___ **QUESTION 112:** C
___ **QUESTION 113:** A

___ **QUESTION 114:** B
___ **QUESTION 115:** B
___ **QUESTION 116:** D
___ **QUESTION 117:** A
___ **QUESTION 118:** B
___ **QUESTION 119:** A
___ **QUESTION 120:** C
___ **QUESTION 121:** D
___ **QUESTION 122:** B
___ **QUESTION 123:** B
___ **QUESTION 124:** A
___ **QUESTION 125:** A

KEEP A RUNNING TALLY OF YOUR CORRECT ANSWERS!

Number correct: ___ / 25

Overall correct: ___ / 125

"It is only fitting that I would follow Marv. For years people have always credited me with being the leader of the Bills. But I can honestly tell you that the real leader of our great team is that man right there, Marv Levy."
— Jim Kelly, Hall of Fame Induction Speech

Chapter Six

Jim Kelly

WHEN BILLS' OWNER Ralph Wilson announced in 2001 that quarterback Jim Kelly would be inducted into the team's Wall of Fame, he added the surprise that Kelly's No. 12 would be the Bills' first-ever retired uniform number.

There were plenty of reasons for the dual honor: Kelly holds virtually every Bills passing record, he led the team to four consecutive American Football Conference championships and an unprecedented four straight Super Bowls, he made five Pro Bowl teams and is among the NFL's all-time best in several categories.

Kelly showed considerable promise ever since emerging from the University of Miami in 1983 as one of that year's legendary quarterback draft class that included John Elway and Dan Marino. After two years in the USFL, Kelly became 12th in NFL passing yardage (35,467), 12th in pass completions (2,874) and 15th in touchdown aerials (237). And on February 2, 2002, he made the Pro Football Hall of Fame— joining Marv Levy, his Bills coach (2001), and Bills predecessors Billy Shaw (1999) and O.J. Simpson (1985).

Kelly passed for more than 3,000 yards in a season eight times. He and Andre Reed became the NFL's third all-time leading aerial combination with 65 touchdown connections from 1986-90. Kelly's other favorite targets in a golden era of passing were James Lofton, Thurman Thomas and Pete Metzelaars.

Starring for the Bills from 1986-96, Kelly completed 60.1 percent of his passes in a 160-game Buffalo career. He finished with a 101-59 regular-season won-lost mark and was 9-8 in post-seasons.

Kelly repeatedly frustrated defenses with a no-huddle offense that rolled up huge yardage and touchdowns. Though the Bills are remembered for losing four straight Super Bowls, almost forgotten is Kelly's last drive of the 20-19 loss to the

Giants in Buffalo's first Super Bowl. He started on the Bills' ten-yard line with 2:16 left and engineered a drive that went 61 yards in eight plays to set up Scott Norwood's 47-yard field goal that was wide right, ending the miracle hopes.

Kelly was the 18th modern-era quarterback selected to the Hall of Fame in Canton, Ohio and the third University of Miami product enshrined behind Ted Hendricks and Jim Otto. Kelly was also the fifth Hall of Famer to wear No. 12—joining Terry Bradshaw, Bob Griese, Joe Namath and Roger Staubach. Kelly, a Pittsburgh product, was the 25th Pennsylvania native enshrined in Canton.

QUESTION 126: In what year did the Bills switch from white to red helmets?
- a) 1982
- b) 1986
- c) 1984
- d) 1985

QUESTION 127: In the AFC realignment of 2002, the Bills remained in the AFC East. But who left for the AFC South?
- a) Baltimore
- b) Cincinnati
- c) Cleveland
- d) Indianapolis

QUESTION 128: Through the 2010 season, how many years have the Bills won at least ten games?
- a) 10
- b) 12
- c) 13
- d) 15

QUESTION 129: Who coached both of the Bills' one-win seasons?
- a) Harvey Johnson
- b) Joe Collier

c) Hank Bullough
d) Kay Stephenson

QUESTION **130:** What are the most points that the Bills scored in any one regular season?
  a) 420
  b) 440
  c) 458
  d) 472

QUESTION **131:** What was an effect of Coach Lou Saban's edict that Bills' wide receivers wear a cage on their helmet so they could block for O.J. Simpson?
  a) Haven Moses objected and was traded to Denver
  b) J.D. Hill liked it, starred as a blocker but never caught a TD pass in 1973
  c) O.J. loved it and broke the NFL's single-season rushing record in '73
  d) All of the above

QUESTION **132:** When O.J. Simpson broke the NFL's one-season rushing record on the 1973 season's final day at New York's Shea Stadium, whose record did he surpass?
  a) Gale Sayers
  b) Walter Payton
  c) Jim Brown
  d) Jim Nance

QUESTION **133:** In how many games did O.J. Simpson run for 200 or more yards?
  a) 5
  b) 6
  c) 4
  d) 3

QUESTION **134:** What was the most rushing yardage that O.J. Simpson rolled up in one game?

a) 273 vs. Detroit
b) 227 vs. Pittsburgh
c) 219 vs. New England
d) 250 vs. New England

QUESTION 135: In 1975, O.J. Simpson set the Bills' record for most touchdowns in a single season. How many did he score?
a) 23
b) 20
c) 15
d) 10

QUESTION 136: Who in the NFL has surpassed O.J. Simpson's 1973 rushing record of 2,003 yards?
a) Eric Dickerson, LA Rams
b) Barry Sanders, Detroit
c) Terrell Davis, Denver
d) All of the above

QUESTION 137: Who was the first Bills' receiver to record 100 catches?
a) Elbert Dubenion
b) Bob Chandler
c) Eric Moulds
d) Andre Reed

QUESTION 138: What controversial decision preceded the Bills' 22-16 "Music City Miracle" Wild Card playoff loss to Tennessee on January 8, 2000?
a) Coach Wade Phillips started quarterback Rob Johnson over Doug Flutie
b) Phillips won the coin toss but decided to kick off
c) Phillips opted to defend the end that left the Bills going against the wind
d) Phillips explained that Flutie had impressive numbers but was too short for postseason play

QUESTION 139: What Bills' star was named AP's Comeback Player of the Year in 1998?
- a) Rob Johnson
- b) Doug Flutie
- c) Eric Moulds
- d) Antowain Smith

QUESTION 140: Who fumbled on the Bills' final play deep in Miami territory as the Dolphins won the January 2, 1999, Wild Card game, 24-17?
- a) Doug Flutie
- b) Antowain Smith
- c) Eric Moulds
- d) Peerless Price

QUESTION 141: How many franchise marks did Drew Bledsoe set in 2002, his first Bills' season?
- a) 8
- b) 10
- c) 12
- d) 7

QUESTION 142: Who holds the Bills' record for TD passes in one season (33)?
- a) Doug Flutie
- b) Drew Bledsoe
- c) Jim Kelly
- d) Jack Kemp

QUESTION 143: How did the Bills obtain quarterback Joe Ferguson in 1973?
- a) Free agent
- b) Third-round draft choice
- c) Trade with Miami
- d) Trade with Cleveland

QUESTION 144: What did 1960s teammates Mike Stratton, John Tracey and Harry Jacobs have in common besides being linebackers?
- a) All were in the insurance business
- b) All had experience in mortuaries
- c) All put their hitting targets in the hospital
- d) They graduated cum laude

QUESTION 145: Who amassed the most Bills' single-season receiving TDs with 11 in 1995?
- a) Eric Moulds
- b) Pete Metzelaars
- c) Andre Reed
- d) Bill Brooks

QUESTION 146: Who was a teammate of Jim Kelly on the USFL New Jersey Generals and the Bills?
- a) Kent Hull
- b) Doug Flutie
- c) Peerless Price
- d) Frank Lewis

QUESTION 147: What was the Bills' highest-rated telecast?
- a) Giants vs. Bills 1991 Super Bowl
- b) Redskins vs. Bills 1992 Super Bowl
- c) Cowboys vs. Bills 1993 Super Bowl
- d) Cowboys vs. Bills 1994 Super Bowl

QUESTION 148: What Bills' receiving record did Andre Reed *NOT* set?
- a) Most consecutive games with a reception
- b) Most receptions
- c) Most receiving yards
- d) None of the above

QUESTION 149: In 1963, who set the Bills' record for most touchdowns in a game with five?

a) Wray Carlton
b) Cookie Gilchrist
c) Jack Kemp
d) Elbert Dubenion

QUESTION 150: Who holds the Bills' records for most rushing attempts in a season and career?
a) O.J. Simpson
b) Joe Cribbs
c) Thurman Thomas
d) Roland Hooks

Chapter Six Answer Key

___ **Question 126:** C   ___ **Question 139:** B
___ **Question 127:** D   ___ **Question 140:** A
___ **Question 128:** C   ___ **Question 141:** B
___ **Question 129:** A   ___ **Question 142:** C
___ **Question 130:** C   ___ **Question 143:** B
___ **Question 131:** D   ___ **Question 144:** A
___ **Question 132:** C   ___ **Question 145:** D
___ **Question 133:** B   ___ **Question 146:** A
___ **Question 134:** A   ___ **Question 147:** D
___ **Question 135:** A   ___ **Question 148:** A
___ **Question 136:** D   ___ **Question 149:** B
___ **Question 137:** C   ___ **Question 150:** C
___ **Question 138:** A

Keep a running tally of your correct answers!

Number correct: ___ / 25

Overall correct: ___ / 150

"When I first walked out onto the practice field as a high school assistant football coach exactly a half-century ago next month, men like Jim Thorpe, Bronko Nagurski, Sid Luckman, and Marion Motley were mythical gods. They still are, and I tread this ground with great reverence for them and for all who reside here. Never did I dream that some day I might be invited to share these same lodgings with them."
— Marv Levy, Hall of Fame Induction Speech

Chapter Seven

Marv Levy

MARV LEVY IS a highly inspirational coach who amassed the best record of any Bills' coach, tied legendary Chicago Bears' coach George Halas as the oldest active NFL pilot at age 72, guided Buffalo teams that won four straight American Football Conference titles and saw the same teams lose a record four straight Super Bowls from 1990-93.

The point often missed by many is the tremendous drive and talent that's necessary to just appear in four consecutive Super Bowls. The Bills accomplished that under Levy and quarterback Jim Kelly—becoming the only team to do so. The Bills nearly won their first Super Bowl after setting a club record for their margin of victory in a 51-3 blowout of Oakland in the 1991 AFC Championship Game. But Scott Norwood's 47-yard Super Bowl field goal attempt with four seconds left was wide right and that left the Bills and their fans stunned in Tampa Stadium.

Levy's otherwise outstanding scoring machine lost the next three Super Bowls to Washington (37-24) and Dallas (52-17 and 30-13), leaving them a special place in NFL history with those four straight appearances. Levy coached the Bills from 1986-97 and his 123 victories are a franchise record. Levy's teams won six division titles and made the postseason in eight of his 11 full Buffalo seasons, making him a natural Pro Football Hall of Fame inductee in 2001. He was NFL Coach of the Year in 1988 and '93 and made the Bills Wall of Fame and the NFL 1990s All-Decade Team.

A little-known fact is Levy outperformed the winningest coach ever in the NFL, Don Shula. Levy is the only coach to own a winning career record against Shula—14-6 in regular seasons and a perfect 3-0 in postseasons.

Levy's total of 154 NFL triumphs left him tenth in league history. He made five AFC title games, winning four, and his 11 postseason wins ranked him fifth in NFL history. He was also Bills' general manager for two years when he retired after coaching the '97 Bills at age 72. The Coe College and Harvard alumnus previously was head coach with Kansas City (1978-82) and the CFL Montreal Alouettes (1973-77, with two league titles) after assistant coaching posts with the Eagles, Rams and Redskins and college head-coaching jobs at New Mexico, California and William and Mary.

The Chicago native and World War II veteran often used historical examples to inspire the Bills, but corrected those who used war metaphors to describe football games. He'd tell them that he fought in a war and there was no comparison. Of the Super Bowl, he declared: "This is not a must-win. World War II was a must-win!"

QUESTION 151: What Bills' star is well remembered for wearing uniform No. 7?
   a) Doug Flutie
   b) Jack Kemp
   c) Rob Johnson
   d) Drew Bledsoe

QUESTION 152: Who rolled up the most Bills' rushing attempts in one game with 39?
   a) Cookie Gilchrist
   b) O.J. Simpson
   c) Joe Cribbs
   d) Jim Braxton

QUESTION 153: How many years has John Murphy been the Bills' radio play-by-play voice since succeeding Van Miller?
   a) 10
   b) 9
   c) 5
   d) 6

QUESTION 154: Mark Kelso, who has been the Bills' radio color analyst for five years, was a Bills' starting free safety for how many years?

- a) 10
- b) 6
- c) 7
- d) 12

QUESTION 155: Who was the 34th quarterback to start in Bills' history?

- a) Doug Flutie
- b) Ryan Fitzpatrick
- c) Trent Edwards
- d) Alex Van Pelt

QUESTION 156: Who kicked the most Bills' PATs in a season?

- a) Scott Norwood
- b) Steve Christie
- c) John Leypoldt
- d) Rian Lindell

QUESTION 157: Who kicked the most Bills' career PATs?

- a) John Leypoldt
- b) Steve Christie
- c) Booth Lusteg
- d) Rian Lindell

QUESTION 158: When the Bills' stadium in Orchard Park was called "Rich Stadium," who was it named after?

- a) One of the All-America Conference Buffalo Bills
- b) Several wealthy Orchard Park citizens
- c) Rich Products president Robert Rich
- d) Erie County's most prominent mayor

QUESTION 159: Why did Coach Lou Saban, after a particularly galling defeat, accuse a Buffalo newspaper of using a "Police Gazette" photo spread?

a) Because on the morning of the game it used a picture of quarterback Dennis Shaw walking his dog in front of his home
b) Because it reported a Bills' player was arrested
c) Because it reported two Bills were in a restaurant after curfew
d) Because it reported one player missed the Bills' flight

QUESTION 160: What Bills' punter had such a gift of gab that he became a noted football analyst on ESPN and later other networks?
a) Spike Jones
b) Paul Maguire
c) Marv Bateman
d) Chris Mohr

QUESTION 161: Who made the most punts (775) over his Bills' career?
a) Paul Maguire
b) Chris Mohr
c) Marv Bateman
d) Brian Moorman

QUESTION 162: What late-1970s Bills' draft choices became fast friends and later team stars?
a) Fred Smerlas and Jim Haslett
b) Tom Cousineau and Jerry Butler
c) Joe Devlin and Ben Williams
d) Mario Clark and Ken Jones

QUESTION 163: What Bills' mid-1970s draft picks and later major disappointments became such dogged holdouts that reporters had to wait all day and into the night in the stadium lobby for their signings to be announced?
a) Reuben Gant and Doug Allen
b) Gary Marangi and Carlester Crumpler

   c) Glenn Lott and Reggie Cherry
   d) Tom Ruud and Bob Nelson

QUESTION 164: In what year were Paul Seymour, Joe DeLamielleure, Joe Ferguson, Wallace Francis and John Skorupan all drafted?
   a) 1977
   b) 1972
   c) 1973
   d) 1974

QUESTION 165: If the Bills had been unable to make O.J. Simpson their top 1969 choice to lead off the NFL draft, what team was in the best position to take him?
   a) Philadelphia
   b) San Francisco
   c) Oakland
   d) New England

QUESTION 166: What Bills' head coach formerly guided the Chicago Bears?
   a) Wade Phillips
   b) Dick Jauron
   c) Gregg Williams
   d) Hank Bullough

QUESTION 167: What was the construction cost of Ralph Wilson Stadium when it opened in 1973?
   a) $20 million
   b) $30 million
   c) $22 million
   d) $25 million

QUESTION 168: When was the Bills' stadium renamed from Rich Products in honor of team founder and owner Ralph Wilson after Rich balked at paying a greatly increased rights fee?

a) 1998
b) 1996
c) 1989
d) 1990

QUESTION 169: How many points did the Bills score combined in their four losing Super Bowls?
a) 68
b) 75
c) 70
d) 73

QUESTION 170: How many points did the Giants, Redskins and Cowboys score collectively against the Bills in those four Super Bowls?
a) 139
b) 140
c) 145
d) 110

QUESTION 171: The Bills' Orchard Park stadium now has a seating capacity of 73,079. But what was the original capacity before it was reduced as part of a lease renewal with Erie County?
a) 75,000
b) 78,010
c) 80,020
d) 82,000

QUESTION 172: The lease agreement included $5.2 million in stadium upgrades with a high definition 88.8-feet by 32.5-feet scoreboard installed in 2007. What else was included?
a) Larger seats and more luxury and club seating
b) Installing scoreboard ribbon boards
c) Removing the 13-year-old Sony JumboTron that had cost an inflation-adjusted $8 million
d) All of the above

QUESTION 173: The stadium's design dictated the field be how many feet below grade while the upper deck is just 60 feet above ground?
   a) 75 feet
   b) 50 feet
   c) 25 feet
   d) 20 feet

QUESTION 174: Which Bills quarterback was the first to throw six touchdowns in one game?
   a) Jack Kemp
   b) Daryle Lamonica
   c) Joe Ferguson
   d) Jim Kelly

QUESTION 175: Who is the oldest Bills' quarterback to ever have a 300-yard aerial game?
   a) Jack Kemp
   b) Doug Flutie
   c) Drew Bledsoe
   d) Joe Ferguson

CHAPTER SEVEN ANSWER KEY

___ **QUESTION 151:** A   ___ **QUESTION 164:** C
___ **QUESTION 152:** B   ___ **QUESTION 165:** A
___ **QUESTION 153:** B   ___ **QUESTION 166:** B
___ **QUESTION 154:** C   ___ **QUESTION 167:** C
___ **QUESTION 155:** B   ___ **QUESTION 168:** A
___ **QUESTION 156:** A   ___ **QUESTION 169:** D
___ **QUESTION 157:** B   ___ **QUESTION 170:** A
___ **QUESTION 158:** C   ___ **QUESTION 171:** C
___ **QUESTION 159:** A   ___ **QUESTION 172:** D
___ **QUESTION 160:** B   ___ **QUESTION 173:** A
___ **QUESTION 161:** D   ___ **QUESTION 174:** D
___ **QUESTION 162:** A   ___ **QUESTION 175:** B
___ **QUESTION 163:** D

KEEP A RUNNING TALLY OF YOUR CORRECT ANSWERS!

Number correct: ___ / 25

Overall correct: ___ / 175

"You can get it done! What's more, you've GOTTA get it done!"
— Lou Saban

Chapter Eight

Lou Saban

LOUIS HENRY SABAN was the Bills' highly successful second coach, serving two tenures and first coming aboard on January 18, 1962, to follow the franchise's first coach, Buster Ramsey. Saban opposed the Bills as coach of the also-new Boston Patriots in the American Football League's initial season of 1960 and, after two winning years that included a 1963 playoff loss to Boston, hit his stride in 1964 and '65. He earned AFL Coach of the Year honors both years after guiding the Bills to consecutive AFL championships.

The 1964 team, led by the quarterbacking of Jack Kemp and Daryle Lamonica and the power running of ex-Canadian Football League star Cookie Gilchrist, compiled a 13-2 record in 1964 and beat San Diego, 20-7, in a War Memorial Stadium collision that featured Mike Stratton's wallop that sent Chargers' star running back Keith Lincoln out of the game injured.

After Gilchrist was dealt to Denver, the Bills were not expected to be as strong in '65. But Wray Carlton became the team's leading rusher and Saban's staunch defense, headed by co-captain Tom Sestak, was dominant in an 11-3-1 campaign. The Chargers, playing at home, were expected to win the title game, but Saban's powerful defense prevailed, 23-0, and the Bills had their second straight league crown.

Saban, featuring a mile-long resume, stunned Bills' fans the following January by resigning to return to the college ranks at the University of Maryland. Saban was succeeded by assistant coach Joe Collier, who won only 13 of 31 games from 1966-68. When Collier was fired following a 48-6 shellacking by Oakland in the '68 season's second game, and replaced by Harvey Johnson, the Bills chose John Rauch as coach with Heisman Trophy winner O.J. Simpson coming aboard as the NFL's No. 1 draft choice. But Rauch incredibly used O.J. more as a decoy than a true rushing star and when he was fired, also succeeded by Johnson, Saban returned in 1972.

Saban, who played for Cleveland Browns coach Paul Brown, had a strong penchant for building teams from the ground up and was known for relying on a strong running game. He did it in his first Buffalo tenure, accenting Gilchrist and he did it in Denver with Floyd Little. Simpson was no exception. Saban discouraged him from going elsewhere and built his offense around the speedy, elusive running back. He also ordered cages be put on the masks of wide receivers, pointing to O.J. and telling them: "There's your meal ticket. Block for him!"

He worked the waiver wire like a genius and assembled a powerful offensive line to block for Simpson and fullback Jim Braxton. Featuring guards Joe DeLamielleure and Reggie McKenzie, it was nicknamed "The Electric Company" for its ability to "turn loose the Juice."

Sure enough, O.J won the NFL rushing crown with 1,251 yards in '72 and then broke the NFL single-season rushing record with 2,003 yards in 1973.

The Bills never won a title in Saban's second tenure, but they made the playoffs in '74 (losing to eventual Super Bowl champion Pittsburgh) and Saban wound up with a two-tenure won-lost record of 68-45-4 when he bid farewell during the '76 season. He was succeeded by former Packers' center Jim Ringo, who went winless the rest of that '76 season.

Saban was a tough-minded coach with a penchant for strong defense, ball-control offense quarterbacked by Kemp, Lamonica and Joe Ferguson, and record running by O.J. Simpson. Saban saved Simpson's career and fittingly, O.J. selected him to handle the introduction when he entered the Hall of Fame to be among football's all-time greats.

No Bills book would be complete without addressing the historic career of O.J. Simpson—it's fitting to do so here, as his career flourished under Saban.

O.J. Simpson is easily the best of Bills' running backs and one of the greatest in NFL history. He broke Jimmy Brown's NFL single-season rushing record with 2,003 yards in 1973 and, though that mark has since been surpassed (first by Chicago Bears' great Walter Payton), it stands as a memorable milestone in Bills' history. He began that '73 season by churning 250 yards in the opener at New England. That's farther than any pro runner had traveled in any one game. He closed that season by becoming the NFL's first 2,000-yard rusher and, in a packed post-game press conference at New York's Shea Stadium he shared the glory with his offensive-unit teammates.

Two years later (1975), the Juice dented the Super Bowl champion Pittsburgh Steelers' armor for 227 yards—a Three Rivers Stadium opener the Steelers would never forget. Considering the quality of competition, that was probably O.J.'s finest effort. In 1976, he rewrote his single-game rushing mark by humbling the Detroit Lions on Thanksgiving Day with 273 rushing yards—and the Lions led the league in defense at the time. O.J. climaxed that season with a staggering 647 yards in his final three games against the Lions, Dolphins and Colts. That equals a full year's output for most NFL backs.

No player put together more 200-yard games than his half-dozen from 1973-76. He's a rare breed who caromed from Heisman Trophy success in 1968 to rushing records and pro football's Hall of Fame. Yet after he finished his career with the San Francisco 49ers, he came upon hard and sad times. He was charged with murdering second wife Nicole in a sensational "Crime-of-the-Century" trial in Los Angeles. He was acquitted, but a civil jury found him responsible for her death. Then he tried to recover stolen memorabilia in a Las Vegas hotel when accompanied by armed acquaintances. He was found guilty and, as this is written, is still serving a long sentence in Reno.

QUESTION 176: Who was the first Bills' running back to gain 1,000 yards in a season?
- a) O.J. Simpson
- b) Wray Carlton
- c) Cookie Gilchrist
- d) Joe Cribbs

QUESTION 177: Who rolled up more 100-yard games rushing (with) 41 than any other player in the 1970s?
- a) O.J. Simpson
- b) Jim Braxton
- c) Joe Cribbs
- d) Curtis Brown

QUESTION 178: Against what opponent did Jim Kelly throw more touchdown passes than any other team?
- a) New England Patriots
- b) New York Jets
- c) Miami Dolphins
- d) Indianapolis Colts

QUESTION 179: Who threw for the most yards (417) in a Bills' defeat?
- a) Doug Flutie
- b) Jack Kemp
- c) Drew Bledsoe
- d) Ryan Fitzpatrick

QUESTION 180: Who joined Travis Henry among Bills' running backs with the most 1,000-yard seasons during the 2000s?
- a) Willis McGahee
- b) Marshawn Lynch
- c) Fred Jackson
- d) All of the above

QUESTION **181:** Andre Reed caught 65 touchdown passes from Jim Kelly. Who among Bills' receivers was a distant second to Reed?
  a) Thurman Thomas
  b) James Lofton
  c) Pete Metzelaars
  d) Jerry Butler

QUESTION **182:** Thurman Thomas caught 472 passes during his Bills' career. How many did he catch during his college career at Oklahoma State?
  a) 50
  b) 100
  c) 85
  d) 2

QUESTION **183:** What Bills' quarterback became the only active NFL player to become an announcer during a Super Bowl?
  a) Jack Kemp
  b) Doug Flutie
  c) Jim Kelly
  d) Daryle Lamonica

QUESTION **184:** Who is the only player in NFL history to lead the league in total yards for four consecutive years?
  a) O.J. Simpson
  b) Thurman Thomas
  c) Cookie Gilchrist
  d) Antowain Smith

QUESTION **185:** During their AFL title seasons of 1964 and '65, how many consecutive games did the Bills' play without allowing a rushing touchdown?
  a) 10
  b) 20
  c) 17
  d) 15

QUESTION 186: Ralph Wilson was a minority owner in what NFL team before he decided to pursue an AFL team?

a) Detroit Lions
b) New York Giants
c) Cleveland Browns
d) Philadelphia Eagles

QUESTION 187: Who was the very successful Bills' "K-Gun" Offense named after?

a) Jim Kelly
b) Keith McKeller
c) Marv Levy's mother
d) Bob Kalsu

QUESTION 188: Where did Ralph Wilson first try to locate his AFL franchise before turning to Buffalo?

a) Atlanta
b) Los Angeles
c) Miami
d) Kansas City

QUESTION 189: In 1961, with one AFL team in danger of folding due to financial problems, Ralph Wilson loaned that team $400,000 to help them continue. What was that team?

a) New York Titans
b) Oakland
c) Dallas
d) San Diego

QUESTION 190: Antoine Winfield was among five 1990s Bills' first-round draft choices at one position. What is it?

a) Running back
b) Linebacker
c) Defensive back
d) Wide receiver

QUESTION **191:** Hall of Fame offensive lineman Joe DeLamielleure began and ended his career with the Bills. But in the middle, he spent a few seasons with what team?
   a) Cleveland
   b) New England
   c) New York Jets
   d) Houston

QUESTION **192:** Joe Ferguson was the first Bills' quarterback to record a 3,000-yard season, doing so in 1979. Then he did it again. In what year did he record his repeat feat?
   a) 1980
   b) 1981
   c) 1982
   d) 1983

QUESTION **193:** What NFL teams play their home games in the state of New York?
   a) New York Jets
   b) New York Giants
   c) Buffalo Bills
   d) All of the above

QUESTION **194:** What quarterback was cut to make roster room for Jim Kelly?
   a) Dennis Shaw
   b) Art Schlichter
   c) Doug Flutie
   d) Alex Van Pelt

QUESTION **195:** Why is Billy Shaw the only Pro Football Hall of Fame member to never play in the NFL?
   a) He was injured in his final season—well before the 1970 AFL-NFL merger
   b) He played and starred only in the AFL and retired long before the merger

c)   He was unfairly snubbed by the NFL
d)   His post-football career prevented him from playing

QUESTION 196: Jim Kelly's No. 12 was the Bills' first uniform number to be retired. Besides O.J. Simpson's No. 32, what other numbers are not worn?
a)   Andre Reed's 83
b)   Thurman Thomas' 34
c)   Bruce Smith's 78
d)   All of the above

QUESTION 197: O.J. Simpson was being considered for the lead role in "The Terminator." Give the best reason why he didn't land the role.
a)   The producers thought audiences wouldn't buy him as a menacing character because of his "nice guy" image
b)   He had a conflict with his Hertz commercial as "The Superstar of Rent-A-Car"
c)   He wanted too much money and a no-cut deal
d)   Shooting conflicted with the start of the Bills' season

QUESTION 198: Who is the winningest quarterback in Bills' history?
a)   Jack Kemp
b)   Joe Ferguson
c)   Jim Kelly
d)   Daryle Lamonica

QUESTION 199: When did the Bills change their team colors to red, white and blue from light blue, white and silver?
a)   1965
b)   1963
c)   1972
d)   1962

QUESTION 200: Who was the first Bills' player ever to gain more than 100 yards rushing and receiving in the same game?

a) Wray Carlton
b) O.J. Simpson
c) Thurman Thomas
d) Cookie Gilchrist

CHAPTER EIGHT ANSWER KEY

___ QUESTION 176: C   ___ QUESTION 189: B
___ QUESTION 177: A   ___ QUESTION 190: C
___ QUESTION 178: B   ___ QUESTION 191: A
___ QUESTION 179: C   ___ QUESTION 192: B
___ QUESTION 180: D   ___ QUESTION 193: C
___ QUESTION 181: C   ___ QUESTION 194: B
___ QUESTION 182: D   ___ QUESTION 195: B
___ QUESTION 183: A   ___ QUESTION 196: D
___ QUESTION 184: B   ___ QUESTION 197: A
___ QUESTION 185: C   ___ QUESTION 198: C
___ QUESTION 186: A   ___ QUESTION 199: D
___ QUESTION 187: B   ___ QUESTION 200: C
___ QUESTION 188: C

KEEP A RUNNING TALLY OF YOUR CORRECT ANSWERS!

Number correct: ___ / 25

Overall correct: ___ / 200

Buffalo Bills IQ

It's time to find out your Bills IQ. Add your total from all eight chapters and see how you did! Here's how it breaks down:

GENIUS BILLS IQ EXCEEDS MARV LEVY	= 190-200
GENIUS BILLS IQ DESTINED TO BE A FIRST BALLOT HALL OF FAMER	= 180-189
GENIUS BILLS IQ IS WORTHY OF A SUPER BOWL TITLE	= 170-179
SUPERIOR BILLS IQ IS WORTHY OF LEGENDARY STATUS	= 160-169
SUPERIOR BILLS IQ MAKES YOU ONE OF THE ALL-TIME GREATS	= 150-159
OUTSTANDING BILLS IQ PLACES YOU AMONG THE TOP PLAYERS	= 140-149
ABOVE AVERAGE BILLS IQ THAT EARNS YOU A NICE PAYCHECK	= 130-139
SOLID BILLS IQ THAT LETS YOU PLAY BALL FOR A LIVING	= 120-129
AVERAGE BILLS IQ LETS YOU WATCH ON THE BIG SCREEN TV	= 000-119

About the Author

JIM BAKER is a sports columnist who covered the Buffalo Bills and the national and regional television-radio beat at *The Buffalo Courier-Express* for 20 years, following graduation from the State University of New York at Buffalo in 1963.

He remained until the newspaper closed in 1983 and then became the Boston Herald's TV-radio columnist from 1983 until his retirement in 2004. He has written five books on sports subjects: "O.J. Simpson," 1974, Grosset & Dunlap. "The Buffalo Bills: O.J. Simpson, Rushing Champion," 1974, Prentice-Hall; "Billie Jean King," 1975, Grosset & Dunlap; "O.J. Simpson's Most Memorable Games," 1978, G.P. Putnam's Sons; and "A View From the Booth: Gil Santos and Gino Cappelletti—25 Years of Broadcasting the New England Patriots," 2008, Rounder Books.

References

Buffalo Bills Press Guides.

National Football League Record & Fact Book.

"O.J. Simpson," By Jim Baker, 1974, Tempo Books.

"O.J. Simpson's Most Memorable Games, By Jim Baker, 1978, Putnam's Sons.

"The Buffalo Bills: O.J. Simpson, Rushing Champion," By Jim Baker, 1974, Stuart Daniels/Prentice-Hall.

About Black Mesa

BLACK MESA IS a Florida-based publishing company that specializes in sports history and trivia books. Look for these popular titles in our trivia IQ series:

- *Mixed Martial Arts (Volumes I & II)*
- *Boston Red Sox (Volumes I & II)*
- *Tampa Bay Rays*
- *New York Yankees*
- *Atlanta Braves*
- *Milwaukee Brewers*
- *St.. Louis Cardinals (Volumes I & II)*
- *Major League Baseball*
- *Cincinnati Reds*
- *Texas Rangers*
- *Boston Celtics (Volumes I & II)*
- *Florida Gators Football*
- *Georgia Bulldogs Football*
- *Texas Longhorns Football*
- *Oklahoma Sooners Football*
- *Texas A&M Aggies Football*
- *New England Patriots*

For information about special discounts for bulk purchases, please email:

black.mesa.publishing@gmail.com

www.blackmesabooks.com

Also in the Sports by the Numbers Series

- *Major League Baseball*
- *New York Yankees*
- *Boston Red Sox*
- *San Francisco Giants*
- *Texas Rangers*
- *University of Oklahoma Football*
- *University of Georgia Football*
- *Penn State University Football*
- *NASCAR*
- *Sacramento Kings*
- *Mixed Martial Arts*

The following is an excerpt from

New York Yankees IQ:
The Ultimate Test of True
Fandom

Tucker Elliot

Available from Black Mesa Publishing

Chapter One

SPRING TRAINING

THIS IS SPRING TRAINING mind you. We're only stretching here. Just trying to get limber after a long winter of chips, couches, remote controls, beverages of choice, and the NFL . . . I mean, there's no sense straining a groin or anything else right out of the box. So we'll just start with some basics—a few of the legends honored by the Yankees with a retired jersey number. No point in sweating bullets over these questions. You don't know these, well, you don't know jack.

THE NUMBERS GAME

QUESTION 1: The Yankees official website calls this legend "combative and daring," and a "brilliant baseball strategist." To honor him the club retired his #1 jersey. Name this legend.

QUESTION 2: The Yankees official website calls this legend "baseball's greatest slugger." This is like teeing up a beach ball, being asked to hit it with a tennis racket, and your only goal is to make contact—but don't worry, it'll get tougher. In the meantime, name this legend and the jersey number retired in his honor.

QUESTION 3: The one word used to describe this player by the Yankees official website is "durable." Yes, another beach ball (at least I hope). Not too many more of these, we'll be done stretching soon. Name this legend and the jersey number retired in his honor.

QUESTION 4: He was once married to Marilyn Monroe . . . *and*, he got to play for the Yankees. Name this legend and the jersey number retired in his honor.

QUESTION 5: The Yankees official website calls this legend "the most feared hitter on the most successful team in history." This is the last beach ball so you better enjoy it. Name this legend and the jersey number retired in his honor.

THE ROOKIES

QUESTION 6: The Yankees have historically won big games—and big awards as well. Which of the following players was the first Yankee in franchise history to win league Rookie of the Year honors?
  a) Bob Grim
  b) Gil McDougald
  c) Tony Kubek

QUESTION 7: Which of the following players was the first Yankee in franchise history to win league Rookie of the Year honors *as a pitcher*?
  a) Dave Righetti
  b) Bob Grim
  c) Stan Bahnsen

QUESTION 8: Joe DiMaggio was eighth in league MVP balloting during his 1936 rookie season. He also won a pennant and batted .346 vs. the Giants as the Yankees won the World Series in six games. DiMaggio won a lot of games and he led the league in a lot of categories throughout his career. He also led the league in one of the following categories during his 1936 rookie campaign. Do you know which one?
  a) 15 triples
  b) 44 doubles
  c) 206 hits

QUESTION 9: Lou Gehrig's .340 lifetime batting average is the second highest in franchise history behind Babe Ruth. Gehrig played 13 games in 1923 and batted .423, and he played ten games in 1924 and batted .500, but his full-fledged rookie season was 1925 when he posted the lowest batting average of his career. Not until 1938, his last full season, did he bat so low again. Do you know what his batting average was in 1925?

  a) .286
  b) .295
  c) .303

QUESTION 10: In 2005, Robinson Cano batted .297 with 14 homers as a rookie for the Yankees. He also scored 78 runs and drove home 62 in only 132 games, numbers that were good enough to earn him a runner-up finish in Rookie of the Year balloting. Which of the following players beat out Cano for top spot in the balloting?

  a) Nick Swisher
  b) Scott Kazmir
  c) Huston Street

THE VETERANS

QUESTION 11: One Yankee veteran made the following statement: "I never wanted all this hoopla. All I wanted is to be a good ballplayer and hit 25 or 30 homers, drive in a hundred runs, hit .280 and help my club win pennants. I just wanted to be one of the guys, an average player having a good season." Can you name the veteran who spoke those words?

QUESTION 12: On April 8, 2003, this veteran, who signed a free agent contract with the Yanks in the offseason, became the first player in franchise history to hit a grand slam during his first game at Yankee Stadium. Can you name him?

QUESTION 13: On January 11, 2005, New York traded Javier Vazquez, Brad Halsey, and Dioner Navarro to an N.L. club in exchange for this veteran pitcher, a future Hall of Famer. Who was the veteran the Yankees traded for? He was 17-8 during his first season in the Bronx.

QUESTION 14: This veteran joined the club after a July 25, 2008, trade with the Pirates—and all he did during his first week was bat .526 (10 for 19) with three doubles, three homers, and ten RBI. Not to mention a 1.158 slugging percentage and a .571 on-base percentage. No wonder he earned league Player of the Week honors. Got any idea at all who this veteran player was?

QUESTION 15: The big surprise here is that when this veteran reliever earned league Player of the Week honors for the last week of May, 2008, it was the first time in his career he earned that recognition. He picked up three saves in four games that week, and gave up just one hit while striking out seven as he improved to 15 for 15 in save opportunities on the season. Who is the veteran closer we're talking about here?

THE LEGENDS

Legends almost always have nicknames. It's no accident, of course, that some of the game's greatest legends—and nicknames—are synonymous with Yankee baseball. Hey, when you're the best . . . right? And if you're a true fan, well, this should be easy. Our first five questions under The Legends category are all nicknames . . . don't blow these, or if you do, at least have enough dignity to not tell anyone.

QUESTION 16: He was "The Yankee Clipper."

QUESTION 17: He was "The Chairman of the Board."

QUESTION 18: He was "Muscles."

QUESTION 19: He was "Scooter."

QUESTION 20: He was "The Old Perfessor."

THE HITTERS

QUESTION 21: This first baseman was one of the most dangerous hitters in the game during his prime, and in 1987 he tied a major league record by hitting a homer in eight consecutive games. Can you name him?

QUESTION 22: Longtime big league manager Rene Lachemann said of this hitter, "I used to tell my pitchers I could get them two strikes on [him] easy, but from then on they were on their own. There's no doubt in my mind that he is the best two-strike hitter in history." This legendary hitter won a lot of batting titles for New York's biggest rival, but he never got a ring until he came to the Bronx. Can you name him?

QUESTION 23: The Hall of Fame's official website calls him "one of the most popular players in major league history . . . a brilliant catcher and dominant hitter." Hector Lopez, also a Yankee, said this player ". . . had the fastest bat I ever saw. He could hit a ball late, that was already past him, and take it out of the park." Who was this dominant hitter?"

QUESTION 24: His decision to sit out a game because of a headache became, in his own words, "the most expensive aspirin in history." That's because by the end of the game, Lou Gehrig had taken his job. Who lost his starting spot to Gehrig that day?

QUESTION 25: This Yankee legend never won a batting title, but he did set a major league record for catchers when he batted .362 for an entire season. Mike Piazza later batted .362 for the Dodgers (he didn't win a batting title either), and as the 2009 season nears its end, the Twins Joe Mauer, who already owns a pair of batting titles, has a chance to eclipse the mark and set a new record . . . but nevertheless, it was this Yankees catcher who set the standard. Can you name him?

THE PITCHERS

QUESTION 26: He was a character, that's for sure. But when he revealed a little bit too much in his 2003 autobiography, the Yankees took the unprecedented step of fining this pitcher a stiff $100,000. It was the biggest team-levied fine in baseball history at the time. Who was the pitcher on the receiving end of it?

QUESTION 27: He was fined an exorbitant amount as well: $50,000. And what was his offense? Unsportsmanlike conduct towards Mike Piazza during the 2000 World Series . . . and it all started with a busted bat. Who was the pitcher on the receiving end of this fine?

QUESTION 28: His nickname was Happy Jack and he was known for using a spitball from time to time. Clark Griffith, his manager, said of the pitch: "I still remember the first day he threw the thing in a regular game. We were playing in Cleveland. He had a tough first inning. They hit him for three runs. He came back to the bench and said, 'Griff, I haven't got my natural stuff today. I'm going to give 'em the spitter the next inning, if it's all right with you.' I told him to go to it, and you know what? He fanned 14. They didn't get another run and we won the game, 4-3." Who is this legendary pitcher?

QUESTION 29: His real name was Vernon though no one called him that, probably not even his mother. You can just call him a Hall of Fame legend who knew how to win, after all, in five trips to the World Series he made seven starts, was 6-0 with a 2.86 earned run average, and won five world championships. And Vernon is better known as . . . come on you know this one, right?

QUESTION 30: He was on the mound on April 22, 1903, as New York played its first game as the Highlanders. The club lost on the road to Washington, 3-1. Do you know who took the mound that day?

THE MANAGERS AND COACHES

QUESTION 31: If I don't ask this question now, you'll spend the rest of the book waiting for it because you know it has to be in here at some point—so here it is, let's get it over with: Billy Martin was once fired by George Steinbrenner after an altercation with a marshmallow salesman in a bar in Minnesota—and that was just *one* of the many times Mr. Steinbrenner fired the Yankee legend (and just one of the many crazy anecdotes about Martin's life and career)—so, exactly how many times did Billy Martin get fired by George Steinbrenner?

QUESTION 32: There have been more legendary coaches and managers for the Yankees than some franchises can boast players, and that's really saying something. And when your team is that rich in talent and tradition you can be sure that other franchises are going to be eager to graze in your pasture, so to speak, hoping some of your success can be transferred elsewhere—say, across town to the *other* New York team. That didn't work out so well in 1961, when the New York Mets introduced this Yankee legend as its first manager—and all he did at the press conference was call the N.L. club "the Knickerbockers." Oops, that's the NBA. Which Yankee legend got confused (and who wouldn't be) when he took the helm for the Mets?

QUESTION 33: Of all the legendary figures to manage the Yankees, he was the first to actually have been born in one of New York's five boroughs. A native of Brooklyn, can you name this legendary Yankee manager?

QUESTION 34: His nickname was "Mighty Mite" but his role in Yankee history is enormous because he managed the club to the first world championship in franchise history, and he also managed the 1927 "Murderers' Row" club. Can you name this legendary Yankee manager?

QUESTION 35: Think about all the athletes who made appearances or who were referenced in the hit TV sitcom *Seinfeld*. Among the ones who were cast and actually appeared on the show are Yankee greats Paul O'Neill, Bernie Williams, and Derek Jeter. And then there was the Yankee manager who also made an appearance on the show. Do you know which Yankee manager it was that made an appearance on Seinfeld?

THE FABULOUS FEATS

QUESTION 36: You know Don Larsen was perfect during Game 5 of the 1956 World Series. And you should also know the two pitchers who were perfect for the Yankees on May 17, 1998, and on July 18, 1999. So go ahead . . . name them.

QUESTION 37: Dodgers star Steve Garvey confessed, "I must admit, when . . . I was sure nobody was looking, I applauded in my glove." What fabulous feat was Garvey admiring?

QUESTION 38: Maris and Mantle garnered a lot of media attention in 1961 when they were chasing Babe Ruth's home run record, but one of their other teammates had an extraordinary season as well, winning the Babe Ruth Award, Major League Cy Young Award, *The Sporting News* Pitcher of the Year Award, and the 1961 World Series MVP Award. Can you name the teammate of Maris and Mantle who had such an extraordinary season in 1961?

QUESTION 39: The Yankees won the pennant in 1976 thanks to this heroic and very fabulous feat. The score was 6-6 in the deciding fifth game vs. the Kansas City Royals when this player got his 11th hit of the series—a walk-off, pennant-winning homer. Who was the hero of the 1976 League Championship

Series that was mobbed at the plate by fans that stormed the field in celebration?

QUESTION 40: On June 17, 1978, Ron Guidry pitched a four-hit shutout vs. California, leading the Yanks to a 4-0 victory. Guidry was so dominant that in one stretch he struck out 12 of 13 batters he faced, and for the game he set a league record for most strikeouts by a lefty. How many Angels did Guidry fan that game?

THE TEAMS

QUESTION 41: Perhaps the most famous team in baseball history is the 1927 "Murderers' Row" club—and not just Yankee history, I mean in *all* of baseball history. There are a lot of reasons that club was so deadly, but one of them is alluded to in this quote: "The way a team plays as a whole determines its success. You may have the greatest bunch of individual stars in the world, but if they don't play together, the club won't be worth a dime." Which member of the 1927 club said those words?
- a) Lou Gehrig
- b) Joe Dugan
- c) Bob Meusel
- d) Babe Ruth

QUESTION 42: And speaking of the 1927 Yankees . . . Babe Ruth, Lou Gehrig, Bob Meusel, Tony Lazzeri, and Earle Combs all batted above .300 for the season. Ruth led the league with 60 homers and Gehrig led the league with 175 runs, but which of those players led the league with 231 hits?
- a) Lou Gehrig
- b) Bob Meusel
- c) Tony Lazzeri
- d) Earle Combs

QUESTION 43: The pitching staff was rather unique for the Yankees in 1983. Ron Guidry led the club with 21 wins (and 21 complete games) while Goose Gossage won 13 and saved 22 out of the pen . . . but can you identify which of the following statements about the 1983 staff is not only true, but also made it truly unique?
  a) Three 20-game winners
  b) Four 15-game winners
  c) Five lefties with 15-plus starts
  d) Seven pitchers with 15-plus starts

QUESTION 44: New York won a lot of games under manager Joe Torre, but 114 wins during the regular season is just ridiculous. Add in 11 more postseason wins and this world championship club was 125-50. During which of Torre's four championship seasons in the Bronx did the Yankees set a franchise record with 114 regular season victories?
  a) 1996
  b) 1998
  c) 1999
  d) 2000

QUESTION 45: For all the awards garnished by Yankee players, only once in franchise history (through 2008) has the Cy Young and Most Valuable Player Award been given to two members of the Yankees during the same season. Which great Yankee team saw two of its players win league Cy Young and MVP honors?
  a) 1958
  b) 1961
  c) 1978
  d) 2001

MISCELLANEOUS

QUESTION 46: Mariano Rivera will go down in history as one of the greatest players to ever wear pinstripes, and for good reason—he's earned that honor. His cousin Ruben Rivera, well, not so much. New York signed the legendary closer's cousin to a one-year contract worth a million dollars in February, 2002, but a month later, during spring training, Ruben Rivera stole a bat and a glove from a teammate's locker and sold the memorabilia for $2,500. Bad, bad decision . . . he got caught, and the Yankees released him and cancelled his contract. Which of the following stars had his bat and glove stolen by Rivera?

  a) Jorge Posada
  b) Bernie Williams
  c) Derek Jeter
  d) Jason Giambi

Question 47: On August 16, 2009, Derek Jeter set a major league record for hits by a shortstop after going 3 for 4 at the plate vs. Seattle. His three hits raised his career total to 2,675 while playing shortstop, two better than the man previously first on that list. Jeter said afterwards, "I just try to be consistent year in and year out. I think if you're consistent, then good things happen." Can you identify the player with 2,673 hits as a shortstop that Jeter surpassed in the record books?

  a) Cal Ripken, Jr.
  b) Omar Vizquel
  c) Luis Aparicio
  d) Robin Yount

Question 48: July 24, 1983: "The Pine Tar Incident." The Yanks led the Royals 4-3 with two outs in the ninth when a two-run homer gave KC the lead. At least temporarily, because the bat used to hit the homer had too much pine tar in places it didn't belong. The batter was called out, and the Yanks won 4-3, at least temporarily, because later that ruling was overturned, the home run was allowed, and the game was replayed from that pivotal moment on—and then the Yanks lost, 5-4. Can you identify the correct list of individuals who were involved in determining the outcome of this famous incident?

    a) Goose Gossage, George Brett, Billy Martin, Tim McClelland, and Lee MacPhail

    b) Goose Gossage, George Brett, Billy Martin, Joe Brinkman, and Bowie Kuhn

    c) George Frazier, George Brett, Billy Martin, Drew Coble, and Lee MacPhail

    d) Dale Murray, George Brett, Billy Martin, Nick Bremigan, and Bowie Kuhn

QUESTION 49: Derek Jeter scored three runs vs. Detroit during Game 1 of the 2006 Division Series. That gave him 84 career postseason runs, moving him ahead of another Yankee legend and into first place on the all-time list. Who held the previous record of 83 runs scored in the postseason?

    a) Bernie Williams

    b) Mickey Mantle

    c) Paul O'Neill

    d) Yogi Berra

QUESTION 50: He said, "I think it's every player's dream to get to the World Series and feel like you've played a part of the team getting there and the team winning." And he certainly earned the right to feel like he contributed to the Yankees success in 1998—he batted 8 for 17 vs. San Diego in the World Series, posted a .824 slugging percentage with two homers, and he fielded the final out of the series to set off a long night of celebrating in the Bronx. Who was the World Series MVP in 1998?

    a) Tino Martinez

    b) Bernie Williams

    c) Paul O'Neill

    d) Scott Brosius

Chapter One Answer Key

Time to find out how you did—put a check mark next to the questions you answered correctly, and when you are done be sure and add up your score to find out your IQ, and to find out if you made the Opening Day roster.

THE NUMBERS GAME
- __ Question 1:   Billy Martin
- __ Question 2:   Babe Ruth, #3
- __ Question 3:   Lou Gehrig, #4
- __ Question 4:   Joe DiMaggio, #5
- __ Question 5:   Mickey Mantle, #7

THE ROOKIES
- __ Question 6:   B – Gil McDougald
- __ Question 7:   C – Stan Bahnsen
- __ Question 8:   A – 15 triples
- __ Question 9:   B – .295
- __ Question 10:   C – Huston Street

THE VETERANS
- __ Question 11:   Roger Maris
- __ Question 12:   Hideki Matsui (okay, so *technically* he was a rookie . . . but given his experience in Japan, for the sake of this question, he was a veteran)
- __ Question 13:   Randy Johnson
- __ Question 14:   Xavier Nady
- __ Question 15:   Mariano Rivera

THE LEGENDS
- __ Question 16:   Joe DiMaggio
- __ Question 17:   Whitey Ford
- __ Question 18:   Mickey Mantle
- __ Question 19:   Phil Rizzuto

_ Question 20:   Casey Stengel

THE HITTERS
_ Question 21:   Don Mattingly
_ Question 22:   Wade Boggs
_ Question 23:   Yogi Berra
_ Question 24:   Wally Pipp
_ Question 25:   Bill Dickey

THE PITCHERS
_ Question 26:   David Wells
_ Question 27:   Roger Clemens
_ Question 28:   Jack Chesbro
_ Question 29:   Lefty Gomez
_ Question 30:   Jack Chesbro

THE MANAGERS AND COACHES
_ Question 31:   5
_ Question 32:   Casey Stengel
_ Question 33:   Joe Torre
_ Question 34:   Miller Huggins
_ Question 35:   Buck Showalter

THE FABULOUS FEATS
_ Question 36:   David Wells & David Cone
_ Question 37:   Reggie Jackson's third homer during Game 6 of the 1977 World Series
_ Question 38:   Whitey Ford
_ Question 39:   Chris Chambliss
_ Question 40:   18

THE TEAMS
_ Question 41:   D – Babe Ruth
_ Question 42:   D – Earle Combs
_ Question 43:   C – Five lefties with 15-plus starts: Ron Guidry, Shane Rawley, Dave Righetti, Bob Shirley, and Ray Fontenot
_ Question 44:   B – 1998

_ Question 45:   B – 1961, Whitey Ford & Roger Maris

MISCELLANEOUS
    _ Question 46:   C – Derek Jeter
    _ Question 47:   C – Luis Aparicio; Vizquel, on the day Jeter broke the record, was still active with the Texas Rangers and finished the day with 2,669 hits as a shortstop, which means Jeter just did beat him in the race to surpass Aparicio at the top of that list
    _ Question 48:   A – Goose Gossage, George Brett, Billy Martin, Tim McClelland, and Lee MacPhail
    _ Question 49:   A – Bernie Williams
    _ Question 50:   D – Scott Brosius

Got your Spring Training total? Here's how it breaks down:

NO DROP STATUS IN FANTASY LEAGUES EVERYWHERE	= 45-50
OPENING DAY STARTER	= 40-44
YOU MADE IT TO THE SHOW	= 35-39
PLATOON PLAYER AT BEST	= 30-34
ANOTHER SEASON IN THE MINORS	= 00-29

Good luck on Opening Day!

www.blackmesabooks.com

Made in the USA
Lexington, KY
21 December 2016